HEMOPHOBULA

THE WANNABE VAMPIRE

Normandy D. Piccolo / Laurence E. Laufer
Scribbled / Doodled

Normandy's Bright Ideas
Florida

HEMOPHOBULA: THE WANNABE VAMPIRE REVAMPED!

Printed in the United States of America
Previous Copyright ©2013, 2015 by Normandy's Bright Ideas
ISBN: 978-0-9859329-5-4

All rights reserved. No part of this book may be used or reproduced in any manner without written permission except in the case of brief quotations embodied in critical articles and reviews. NormandysBrightIdeas.com

Second Edition
~
10 9 8 7 6 5 4 3

Just keep Trying.

FANGED - HISTORIA 101

Before the surreal tale of Hemophobula can be told, let's begin with a short history lesson on vampires, particularly the most recognized one of them all.

For centuries, young wannabe vampires have longed to be like Transylvania's most notorious neck nibbler, Count Dracula. He is tall, handsome and a bit mysterious. He can become a bat whenever he feels like it, too. The werewolf on the other hand, needs a full moon in order to change. Frankenstein requires a jolt of electricity and a cup of coffee to wake-up. The zombie needs a brain to tell him what to do. And, the Mummy has to wait for toilet paper to go on sale so he can afford to wrap up and leave the tomb.

Dracula is the coolest vampire, ever. No, seriously. He's really cold to the touch, especially his feet. They feel like ice cubes, popsicles and a frozen pizza rolled up into one giant 'Burrrrrr-ito'. The famous fang face typically snores inside a grimy coffin until sunset, when he arises to hunt. Dracula always enjoys sipping on his favorite drink, a bloody Mary. Every non-vampire girl he seems to meet is named Mary. Go figure.

After learning all of that, can you blame a star-struck O Positive plasma guzzler for going a bit batty over the captivating caped cross hater?

DID YOU KNOW THESE WEIRD FACTS ABOUT FANGED BLOOD-SUCKERS?

ONE: Vampires loathe garlic, even the Italian vampires. "Brutto!" (Nasty) While garlic is delicious and healthy to eat, it causes bad breath and immediately repels a vampire.

TWO: Vampires love the element of surprise. They get hurt and insulted when not invited inside someone's home, especially for a surprise party. Vampires can be so sensitive sometimes.

THREE: Vampires live in constant fear of the vampire slayer. If a vampire's non-beating heart gets staked, 'POOF!' they become a pile of ash. A walk in the park on a sunny day will do the same thing. Luckily, the pale look is making a come-back.

FOUR: Crosses are like hitting a brick wall. No wonder a vampire who won't quit trying to move towards one ends up getting a nose job.

FIVE: Vampires have OCD (Obsessive Compulsive Disorder) especially when it comes to shoelaces. Vampires are obsessed with untying every knot they see. If you find your shoelaces mysteriously untied, look around, a vampire may have done it.

SIX: Vampires have to count. They love to do this with seeds and grains. They are really good at math and are probably the only ones on the planet who actually use algebra. How do you think 'The Count' got his job on Sesame Street? "Von (one)...Do (two)...Tree (three)! Ba-Ha-Ha-Ha-Ha!"

SEVEN: Because vampires are so pale, they can easily be mistaken for marshmallows at Monster Bonfires and get roasted by accident, 'Tssssss!' which is why they are afraid of fire.

EIGHT: Vampires cannot stand the smell of cheap drugstore, 'Eau De La Pew-Pew' perfume, as they call it. The stuff smells like a cross between a skunk, dog poo and a barrel of rotten apples. One sure way to keep a vampire away from your neck is to wear it. But be warned, you'll probably keep everyone else away, too.

ABOUT THE BOY

Sillyvania is a town nestled in the mountains of Romania, next to Transylvania. While Transylvania got on the map for Dracula, the Bran Castle, fortified churches and amazing caves, Sillyvania unfortunately became known for something a bit off-beat.

Sillyvania was rarely spoken of, let alone visited by tourists, until the most disastrous wannabe vampire awoke from a crypt one dark, stormy eve. His name was Hemophobula. Hemophobula was no exception to wanting to be a famous vampire like Count Dracula, but perhaps he should have been.

HEE MO FOE BU LA

Hemophobula was the opposite of everything a blood chugalugging vampire was supposed to be. He was a squirt, a pee-wee, a teeny weeny boy with bucktoothed fangs. He constantly tripped over his extra-extra-small black cape and sounded like a stuttering chipmunk on helium when he spoke...a far cry from being scary and cool like Dracula.

But, short legs, a squeaky voice and big teeth were the least of Hemophobula's problems. You see, Hemophobula had arisen from the dead with an odd phobia. The sight of blood and anything colored red caused him to faint. What bloodcurdling vampire does that?

The issue was first discovered after Hemophobula squished a hungry mosquito on his pasty white leg. He saw the blood splatter. His eyes rolled backwards. He leaned to the left. He leaned to the right. He leaned to the left again and then fainted, face first into a patch of stinky swamp weeds.

SCHOOL'S IN SESSION

Hemophobula, phobic or not, was bound and determined to be like Count Dracula. So, he signed up for classes at the most popular vampire school in the entire world. He was immediately accepted and could not wait to begin his first day.

SUCKA UR BLOOD ACADEMY

"where they do indeed bite."

Suckaurblood Academy sits beside Hallow Hill, the largest cemetary in Sillyvania. Teachers use Hallow Hill to show hopeful vampires how to hide behind headstones to escape the ruthless Slayer and occassional crazy, autograph seekers.

Students are also shown how to choose the right coffin to sleep in. Comfort and style, even for the undead, is important. A vampire simply cannot be up all night hunting if he or she has been up all day because of a lumpy, bumpy casket. Vampires must always look their best in order to attract a decent meal. Dark eyes are rather alluring and mysterious, but dark circles under the eyes are quite frightening. Some vampires use cucumbers under the eyes to temporarily fix this problem until the right coffin comes along.

Inside the academy, fang-bearing pupils are taught how to: turn themselves into mist, how to duck from thrown Holy Water, how to avoid sunlight in a shady park on a windy day, how to bite into a neck so as to not draw attention and how to get invited into a stranger's home for dinner...so to speak.

Despite countless obstacles, especially fainting at the sight of blood and the color red, Hemophobula was determined to become the world's next famously feared vampire.

"Dra...Dra...Dracula's like a thousand plus years old. He's gonna re...re...retire soon and then I'll make my move.." Hemophobula closed his eyes and then daydreamed of such a day.

But, in order for his daydream to become a reality, Hemophobula would have to pass all of Miss Fangloosa's classes at Suckaurblood Academy, with flying dark colors.

So, begins the amusing legend of Sillyvania's very own, Hemophoblua: The Wannabe Vampire.

COFFIN CLASS

"Tonight, my precious leeches, we shall learn the correct way to rest one's body when laying inside a coffin. Our bed", Miss Fangloosa said, baring two crooked, sharp, yellow colored fangs. The curious class stared straight ahead.

"Hemophobula!" Miss Fangloosa shrilled forth.

"Ye...ye...yes, Miss Fangloosa", he nervously stammered back.

"Step forward and climb inside the casket, please." She then pointed at a dusty, decrepit wooden box at the front of the classroom next to her desk.

Hemophobula swallowed hard, "*Gulp!*" as he slowly stumbled his way towards the rickety coffin.

"Well, get in. We haven't got all night", Miss Fangloosa said before nudging Hemophobula forward.

"Ye...ye...yes, Miss Fangloosa." Hemophobula carefully climbed in and sat, trembling.

"Lay back, Hemophobula", Miss Fangloosa ordered.

He hesitated, so Miss Fangloosa reached over and pushed Hemophobula down, flat onto his back. A puff of brown dust filled the air.

Hemophobula sneezed, "AChoo!"

"A vampire should never do things halfway. Isn't that right, Hemophobula?"

"Ye...ye...yes, Miss Fangloosa." He sneezed again, "AChoo!"

"Now, cross your arms over your chest, like this, Hemophobula." Everyone watched as Miss Fangloosa placed her right hand in the middle of her chest and then placed her left hand on top of it.

Hemophobula did as he was told and then sneezed again, "AChoo!"

"A vampire must be inside his or her coffin before the sun rises or else!" Without warning, Miss Fangloosa shouted, "DAYLIGHT is here!" and then slammed the coffin lid down, leaving Hemophobula trapped inside.

Darkness!

Panic!

Sneezing began!

"Le…le…let me out of here!" Hemophobula cried, as he banged on the coffin lid with his hands. "AChoo! Le…le..let me out of here! I need my inhaler!" He banged on the lid again.

Miss Fangloosa pounded her fist down and hissed, "Silence! A vampire must always display bravery no matter the situation."

"But the dust! The ma…ma…mold! My allergies! The walls are closing in, Miss Fangloosa! I can't ba… ba…breathe! Oh no!" Hemophobula whimpered out as his nose began to itch like never before. I have to…I have to….sna…sna…sna….sna…SNEEZE!"

"Ahhhhh-Chooo!"

Hemophobula's powerful sneeze blew the lid right off of the wooden coffin. It spun over Miss Fangloosa's head before landing with a loud thump on top of her desk. The class erupted in laughter. Miss Fangloosa sneezed so hard, the bun in her hair fell loose. "Achoo! Achoo! Achoo!"

As both student and teacher continued to sneeze, Miss Fangloosa yanked Hemophobula out of the coffin by the scruff of his neck and reattached the lid. She then invited another student, Julian, to step forth and show how a vampire is supposed to enjoy sleeping, not sneezing and having panic attacks while locked inside their coffin.

HOMEWORK MIS-TAKE

"Last evening, my precious leeches, I spoke about a piece of wood with a very sharp point called a wooden stake. It is often used by a Vampire Slayer in a fight. If the sharp point pierces your heart, you will go from a vampire to a pile of dust." She then snapped her fingers and added, "Just like that!"

The students' eyes grew wide over Miss Fangloosa's scary warning, except for Hemophobula, whose eyeballs naturally bugged out of his head.

"I asked that you each bring a stake to class tonight as part of your homework assignment. It is so important that you each learn how to avoid being stuck by one. Please carefully pull out your stakes now, my precious leeches. I don't want any accidental dustings."

One by one, the wannabe vampires carefully reached into their desks, backpacks and back pockets, and brought forth their sharp wooden stakes.

Hemophobula opened his brown paper bag, began to unwrap the contents and muttered, "Oh no! I brought the wrong **stake**-this is my pet wolf's dinner **steak**!"

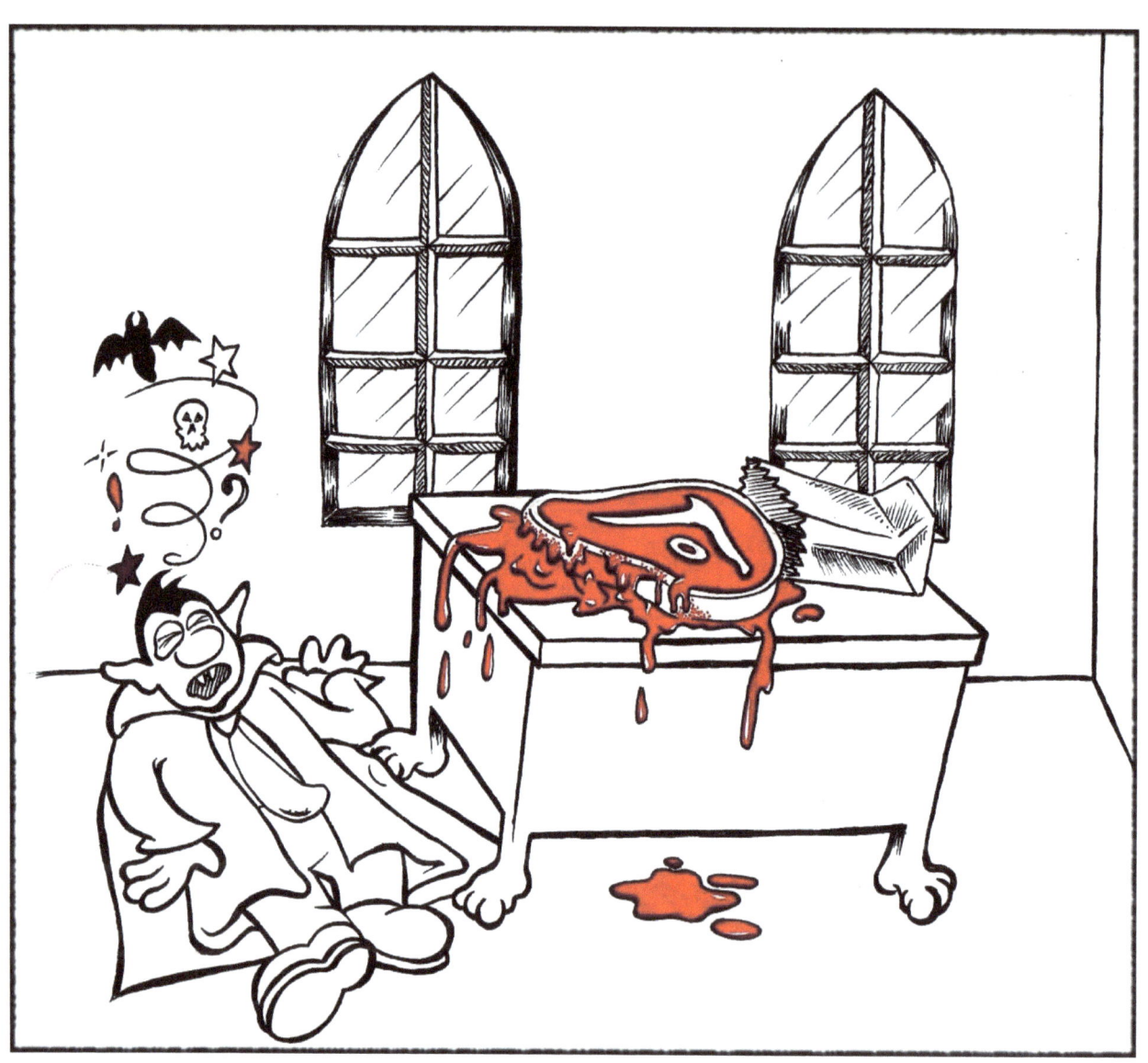

A small droplet of blood dripped from the meat, down onto his desk.

Hemophobula's eyeballs zeroed in on it.

Hemophobula leaned to the left…then to the right….then left again. His eyes rolled into the back of his head.

He fainted.

I VANT TO...

"Hemophobula and Crimson! Please step forward", Miss Fangloosa ordered.

Hemophobula immediately grew weak in the knees at the sight of his beautiful classmate, Crimson,

He grabbed the side of his desk for balance. For a vampire who faints at the sight of blood, and the color red, his reaction to Crimson made perfect sense. Crimson had decided to set herself apart from the other potential Countesses at Sukaurblood Academy by dressing in dark red only. She had dark red hair, put on dark red lipstick, dark red shoes, dark red nail polish and she wore a crushed velvet dark red dress.

"Black makes me look sooooo undead", she always complained.

The sea of Crimson's fashion waves caused Hemophobula to lean to the left and then right again.

He fainted.

"Hemophobula!" Miss Fangloosa shouted.

"Ye…ye…yes, Miss Fangloosa", he nervously stammered back, while picking himself up off of the floor.

"I want you to walk up to Crimson and tell her the following in your most serious voice possible.

"Ye…ye…yes, Miss Fangloosa", he replied in a high-pitched voice.

"I want you to look deep into her eyes and say, 'I Vant to Sock Your Blood'." Miss Fangloosa looked at the class and added, "A vampire must always be in control of his or her victim. Making eye contact is one of such ways."

Hemophobula stood before Crimson while continuing to fight the urge to faint.

"Duh! I'm waiting maggot brain", an impatient Crimson snapped out as she began filing her dark red fingernails into ten sharp points.

A three-foot tall Hemophobula glided up to the six-foot tall Crimson where he tried his best to make eye-contact. He wound up with a kink in his neck instead.

"Well, vein drainer?" she replied, glaring down at the shrimp standing before her. Crimson wanted to burst out laughing, but if she did, she was certain Miss Fangloosa would give her an "F". Knowing she needed to pass this class, Crimson focused on filing her nails.

Hemophobula closed his eyes and in a high-pitched voice stuttered out, "Crim…Crim… Crimson. I van..van…vant to sa…sa…sa…"

"Oh! This is tragic, Miss Fangloosa", she cried out.

"I know Crimson. I know. Believe me I do", Miss Fangloosa replied, looking on in disbelief at a sputtering Hemophobula.

"sa…sa…sa…Crimson…I van…van…Oh!" He continued with both eyes still tightly closed.

"No! Not the babbling immortal," she whined, raising her hand. "Me! Miss Fanglossa! I broke a fingernail. See?"

Miss Fangloosa palmed her own forehead. "Take your seat, Crimson."

"Yes, Miss Fangloosa.."

"Crim...Crim...Crimson. I van....van...vant to sa.....sa...sa...drink your blood, ok?" Hemophobula then opened his eyes and was stunned to find a bewildered Miss Fangloosa in Crimson's place.

The class laughed out loud. Hemophobula turned red from embarrassment and almost fainted. "That statement is incorrect, Hemophobula! I want you to take this mirror, return to your desk and practice saying, 'I Vant to Sock Your Blood' until dawn if you hope to pass this class.

"Bu...bu...but I can't practice in front of a mirror, Miss Fanglossa."

Miss Fangloosa placed a hand on each hip and snapped back, "And why not, young fledgling?"

Vamp....vamp...vampires don't have reflections, Miss Fangloosa. We are invisible, remember?"

"Well Count Dracula can say 'I Vant to Sock Your Blood' and so too, will you." She handed over her compact with the mirror inside. "Scoot!"

Hemophobula stared at the blank mirror and could be heard mumbling, "Ma...ma...mirror, ma...ma...mirror on the wall, I van...van...vant to sa...sa...sa...drink your blood, that is all."

TABLE FOR ONE

The hungry wannabe vampires flocked to Suckauurblood Academy's ghoulish cafeteria for a midnight snack. They could hardly wait to sink their sharp fangs into bagged pints of O positive blood. Everyone happily slurped on the bittersweet plasma, except for Hemophobula. Remember, blood makes him faint, so Hemophobula's Mom packed a lunch full of his favorite treats to eat.

Hemophobula set a brown lunch bag on the table and proudly pulled out the following food items: garlic bread, garlic pizza, garlic soup, grilled garlic slices and a thermos full of garlic juice. He innocently held up a container of cream colored stuff and asked, "Would anyone like to ta...ta...taste my Ma....Ma...Mom's grilled garlic slices? They're very tasty."

The 'Blood-fueled Slurpfest' came to an abrupt halt as the wannabe vampires leaped up from their chairs and immediately scattered from the table, stumbling over each other, trying to flee Hemophobula's garlic spread.

"Ga...ga...guys?" Hemophobula asked, looking around the cafeteria. He was surrounded by abandoned, dripping pints of blood. His eyes zoned in and out on the half-drained bags. Hemophobula leaned to the left....then right....then left again.

THUD!

He landed, face first on his plate of grilled garlic slices.

OH BATS!

The class had transformed themselves into flying vampire bats. Miss Fangloosa even joined in on the fun, too. Everyone was flapping their wings and zooming around the classroom, except Hemophobula, of course.

"Dra....dra...drats!" He huffed. "Dra....Dra...Dracula always makes becoming a ba...ba...bat look as easy as von...do...tree."

Hemophobula continued trying, but the more he strained, the redder his face became. This was the only noticeable change so far. But, he was not ready to quit. The brave little wannabe vampire kept going until it finally happened. Only what happened was not expected, but at the same time not entirely unexpected considering Hemophobula's involvement.

Hemophobula had strained so hard, his black cape ripped at the seams. Between the sound of tearing fabric and the cape's exposed red satin interior, poor little Hemophobula thought he had ripped himself wide open and that his guts were about to spill onto the floor for everyone to slip- and-slide in.

Hemophobula leaned left....then right...then left again. His eyeballs rolled back into his head. He fainted.

MYSTIFIED

Miss Fangloosa stood before the class, looking as she always did: dressed in black with her hair in a tight bun resting on the back of her pale neck. Then, in the blink of an eye, Miss Fangloosa switched herself into a misty white cloud.

While hovering up and down in front of the classroom, she echoed, "Should a vampire become trapped, he or she can change into a cloud of mist and simply float away from the danger." She then demonstrated by drifting around the classroom.

The impressed class blurted several *'Ooh'* and *'Ahh'* sounds.

Miss Fangloosa returned to the front of the class and resumed her normal appearance. "Now my precious leeches, I want each of you to practice changing into mist just as I did." She then shouted, "Crimson!"

"Yes, Miss Fangloosa?"

"Close all of the windows first, please", Miss Fangloosa ordered. "I don't want anyone to accidentally wander away." She raised her left eyebrow in Hemophobula's direction. He swallowed hard, 'Gulp!'

"Yes, Miss Fangloosa." Crimson set her nail file down and closed the windows.

One by one the wannabe parasites turned themselves into clouds of mist and floated freely about the classroom. Hemophobula was having some trouble. Not surprising. He stressed, strained and concentrated. After endless failures at Suckauublood Academy, success appeared to have finally landed in his lap.

"Che…Che…Check me out, Miss Fangloosa! I did it! I cha…cha…changed into a ma…ma…misty cloud!" He cried while floating over a laboratory table covered with large glass jars.

"Fangtastic, Hemophobula! Fangtastic!" Miss Fangloosa praised.

The air-conditioning turned on. Rushing air from the vent suddenly blew Hemophobula towards a bright glowing red exit sign. The sign cast its red glow onto Hemophobula's misty white form. He muttered, "Re…Re…Red!" as his eyes rolled forward, then back into his head before he dropped out of the air, back in his original form.

A glass jar rolled back and forth, 'Tink-Tink-Tink!' before coming to a rest. Hemophobula was now jammed head first inside it, his cape and lower half hanging out.

In the misty haze of the classroom, all could hear the crazed and shrill voice of Miss Fangloosa screaming, "NOT AGAIN, HEMOPHOBULA!"

Holy Meltdown

"…and so my precious leeches remember, touch so much as one drop of Holy Water, and you are certain to melt into a puddle of watery goo", Miss Fangloosa warned, as she carefully set a water-filled syringe on top of her desk. "Always be sure to carry a miniature umbrella inside your cape for just such occasions." She tucked her umbrella away and cried out, "Hemophobula!"

"Ye…Ye…Yes, Miss Fangloosa?"

"Come to the front of the class and repeat the lesson I just gave on the dangers of Holy Water and how to use an umbrella to avoid getting splashed."

"Ye…Ye…Yes, Miss Fangloosa."

Hemophobula was nervously walking up to Miss Fangloosa's desk when, without warning, his left foot tripped up his right foot, causing him to lose his balance. He fell forward and unfortunately for Miss Fangloosa, his hand landed on the syringe full of Holy Water.

Miss Fangloosa tried to reach inside her cape for her mini-umbrella, but it was too late.

The syringe shot forth a stream of Holy Water.

It landed on Miss Fangloosa's wretched face.

The normally composed teacher immediately began to scream, steam and melt, as the horrified fanged class looked on.

"Hemophobula! I'm wasting…away! Dis…solving! Liquify….ing! Class is disssssss…..mi…. ssssssssed!" She shrieked before becoming a puddle of goo.

"Wow! She wasn't kidding about that puddle thing", Crimson said, while trying to see her reflection in Miss Fangloosa's melted goo. "Oh well, I guess I have more time now to file my nails."

Thankfully Miss Fangloosa reappeared twenty-four hours later with some help from the witches at Broomstick Academy right down the road.

(For melting the teacher)

OH BATS! PART 2

Hemophobula begged Miss Fangloosa for permission to retake the 'Bat Exam'.

"I know I ca…ca…can pass it this ti…ti…time, Miss Fangloosa."

"All right, Hemophobula…" an unconvinced Miss Fangloosa sighed. "Let's see if you can indeed change yourself into a vampire bat." She then muttered, "Preferably before the rising of the sun."

Hemophobula happily nodded his head up and down really fast in a 'Yes' gesture. All Miss Fangloosa saw in this moment of eagerness was what appeared to be a flailing black moth blinded by a light.

"You will se…se…see, Miss Fangloosa. I am going to do it this ti…ti…time. I will change into a vampire ba…ba…bat and pass this class."

Miss Fangloosa sat down behind her desk. "Shall we begin?"

In typical Hemophobula fashion, he stressed, strained, flexed and strained some more.

Something began happening. Hemophobula felt weird. His body tingled. His head quickly shrank causing his eyes to pop outward. His arms drew in close to his body and became web like, as his cape disappeared. Hemophobula was suddenly light as a feather.

"Lo…lo…look, Miss Fangloosa", Hemophobula cried, now flying freely around the classroom. "I did it! I changed into a vampire ba…ba…bat!"

Miss Fangloosa was stunned. She burst into a huge fang-bearing grin, and in a rare display of emotion shouted, "Bravo, Hemophobula! Bravo!"

But, as usual, the joy of a possible victory for Hemophobula was about to come undone. Hemophobula spotted an object on Miss Fangloosa's desk. For some odd reason, he found himself drawn to it and hypnotically swooped down, buck-toothed fangs bared, seeking that big delicious bite of success as a vampire.

CRUNCH…BITE!

"AARGH", he mumbled, "That lo…lo…looks like blood." as he continued to stare at red juice oozing from the two puncture marks he just made.

Hemophobula had bitten into a rotten pomegranate fruit that vampire hopeful, Julian, had given to Miss Fangloosa for her pet vulture, Balderdash.

Hemophobula began to feel faint. He quickly flapped his wings away from the bleeding fruit, and in a state of confusion, mostly due to his eyes continually rolling back and forth in his head, flew straight into the chalkboard.

Bat-formed Hemophobula, fell to the floor.

Miss Fangloosa groaned, slapped her hand onto her forehead and shouted, "Hemophobula! You dingbat! You turned yourself into a fruit bat instead!" She then peeled the disoriented bat up off the floor and flailed him with her hands a few times until he changed back.

CROSS IN THE ROAD

Despite the many, many, many, many, many, many failings and mishaps in Miss Fangloosa's classes, the administration at Suckaurblood Academy, decided to let Hemophobula graduate. They claimed it was due to his hard work and determination to be the best vampire in Sillyvania. But, truth be told, the school could not afford any more accidents…basically Hemophobula himself.

So, on October 30th, at the stroke of midnight, and the beginning of all Hollows-Eve, October 31st, Hemophobula would graduate and become:

COUNT HEMOPHOBULA

Hemophobula was really excited to finally be a Count, like his undead celebrity idol, Dracula. But, in typical Hemophobula fashion, he was running late. He ran late to his own funeral. He was certain to miss the graduation ceremony if he did not hurry. A shortcut was the only way.

"Eureka! Suckaurblood Academy is ju…ju…just on the other side of this railroad cro…cro…crossing. I will be on ti…ti…time for once in my after life."

Hemophobula took a step forward.

"Ouch!" He cried. "I can't mo…mo…move forward. It's li…li…like hitting an invisible wall." He tried again. "Ouch! That hurts my nose!"

Hemophobula was confused, stuck and running out of time. "Why can't I mo…mo…move forward?" he asked. He tried again. "Ouch!"

Then the answer came to him. Miss Fangloosa had taught a class on crosses and their power to stop vampires from moving forward. Hemophobula was standing before a railroad cross-buck warning sign. The sign was preventing him from crossing over the tracks and getting to his graduation on time.

"Dra…Dra…Drats!"

A frustrated Hemophobula turned and headed back to the original path he always took to Suckaurblood Academy, walking and tripping the entire time.

Hemophobula heard the faint voice of Count Dracula, calling his name, "Count Hemo…pho…buuuuu…la. Count Hemo…pho…buuuuu…la. No? Alright, moving on. Countess Crrrrrrrr…immmmmm…..sssssssssson."

Countess Crimson marched across the stage to receive her diploma with a just arrived, panting Count Hemophobula, hanging onto her cape, trailing behind.

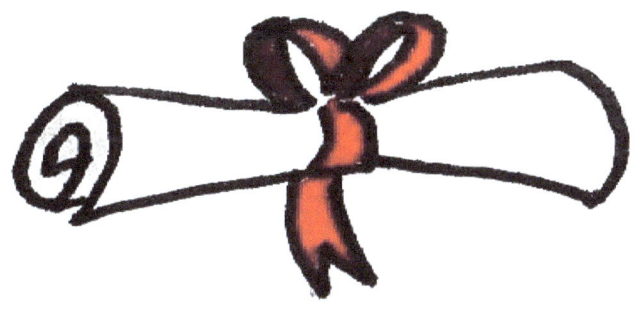

Diploma Received!

DIGITAL DUST

Hemophobula nearly missed walking across the stage to receive his diploma and shake Count Dracula's cold hand. But, that was all worms in the dirt, for Hemophobula had officially graduated and would now be known from here on out as:

COUNT HEMOPHOBULA

"Fellow cla…cla…classmates?" He asked.

"What do you want now, maggot brain?" Countess Crimson asked, filing her nails, as usual.

"I would like to ta…ta…take a picture of the class for my scra…scra…scrapbook, ok?"

"Ummm. You can't take a picture of us, death-breath", Countess Crimson snapped back.

"Why not?" A confused Hemophobula asked with a camera in hand.

Countess Crimson sighed, "Because vampires don't show up on film. Everyone knows that. Duh!"

"But I have a new di…di…digital camera. You all will show up on it. You'll se…se…see, Crim…Crim…Crimson."

"If you say so. Come on everyone gather around for clumsy corpse and his magical camera." Crimson sarcastically ordered.

The graduating class of Suckaurblood Academy stood together, arms wrapped around each other, fangs showing, diplomas displayed, waiting for Count Hemophobula to take their picture. The group of newly ordained Counts and Countesses were really excited. This would be the first time each vampire would get to see what he or she looked like to the world. Mirrors and camera film had been useless until now. The suspense was almost too much to contain.

"Oh, I hope my hair looks alright", Countess Crimson whined.

Hemophobula shouted, "Ok. On the co…co…count of three!"

He then took the picture.

"Hey! Where di…di…did everyone go?" Count Hemophobula asked while staring down at piles of dust, caps, gowns and diplomas.

The answer came when he noticed a tiny flashing red light on top of the digital camera.

"Uh-oh!" he cried, "I forgot to turn off the captured sunlight flash before taking the picture." His eyes began zeroing in on the red light. He leaned to the left….then right….then left again.

He fainted.

The digital camera rolled out of his hand and, snapped one last picture.

Rip Miss Fangloosa.

TEACHER WANTED

TO HELP TEACH WANNABE VAMPIRES AT SUCKAURBLOOD ACADEMY. MUST BE PATIENT, WILLING TO BE MELTED, STAKED, HAVE COFFIN LIDS FLY OVER YOUR HEAD, AND TOLERATE THE SMELL OF GARLIC, AMONG OTHER MISHAPS AND SHENANIGANS WHILE STUDENT HEMOPHOBULA IS ATTENDING CLASSES. THIS IS A PERMANENT JOB UNLESS YOU GET ACCIDENTALLY DUSTED LIKE THE LAST TEACHER DID. PLEASE APPLY FOR THIS POSITION BEFORE SUNRISE.

Diploma Revoked!

"Dra...Dra...DraTS!"

HEMOPHOBULA'S

RECIPES

Garlic Soup

15 Cloves of garlic chopped
1 Chopped potato (Skin optional)
1 Cup of chopped carrots
1 Cup of chopped onion
6 Cups of chicken broth
1 Cup of milk
2 Tbsp. of butter
1 Tbsp. of extra-virgin olive oil
1 Tbsp. of Rosemary (freshly chopped or dried)
2 Tbsp. of Parsley (freshly chopped or dried)
2 Bay Leaves (fresh or dried)
½ Tsp. of sea salt
½ Tsp. of black pepper

In a frying pan sautee the onions and garlic in the olive oil until slightly brown. Add them to a pot which contains the remaining ingredients. Cook over a medium/low heat until the carrots and potatoes are soft. Approximately 30-35 minutes. Serve with parmesan cheese s, bacon bits, crackers or croutons sprinkled on top.

Garlic Juice

Go to the grocery store and buy it…easier and less messy than trying to make it from scratch.

Grilled Garlic Slices

3 Clove of garlic sliced medium-thin
2 Tbsp. of melted butter
Dash of sea salt and black pepper

Place the garlic slices, coated in the melted butter and seasoned with salt and pepper, onto a piece of aluminum foil and put it on the grill. Cook until the slices are a desired brown color. Eat them as is or you can place them on top of a slice of toasted bread and then garnish with parmesan cheese.

Garlic Pizza

10   Sliced cloves of garlic
1   Pre-made dough pizza crust
1   Can of pizza sauce
1 ½ Cups of shredded mozzarella cheese

Preheat the oven at 450 degrees (unless the pizza dough you are using states another oven temperature/cooking time frame to use). Spread the pizza sauce over the crust. Sprinkle the mozzarella cheese evenly on top of the sauce. Add/scatter the garlic slices. Feel free to add any additional toppings you like; mushrooms, pepperoni, olives, etc.. Bake 8-12 minutes.